Ukrainian Girls

Hot Sexy Ukrainian Lingerie Girls Models Pictures

By **PHOTO ART LOVER**

Copyright © Ukrainian Girls

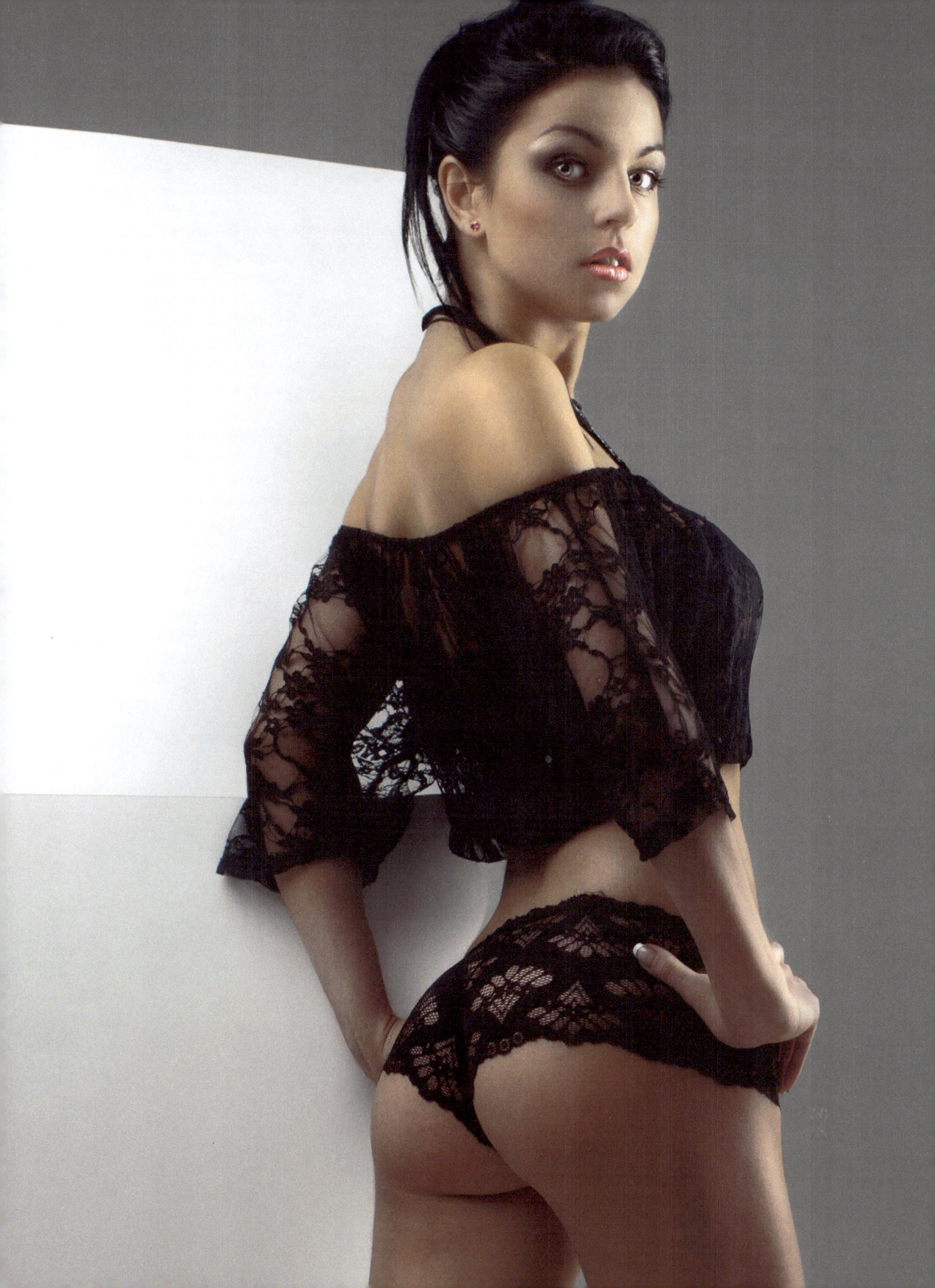

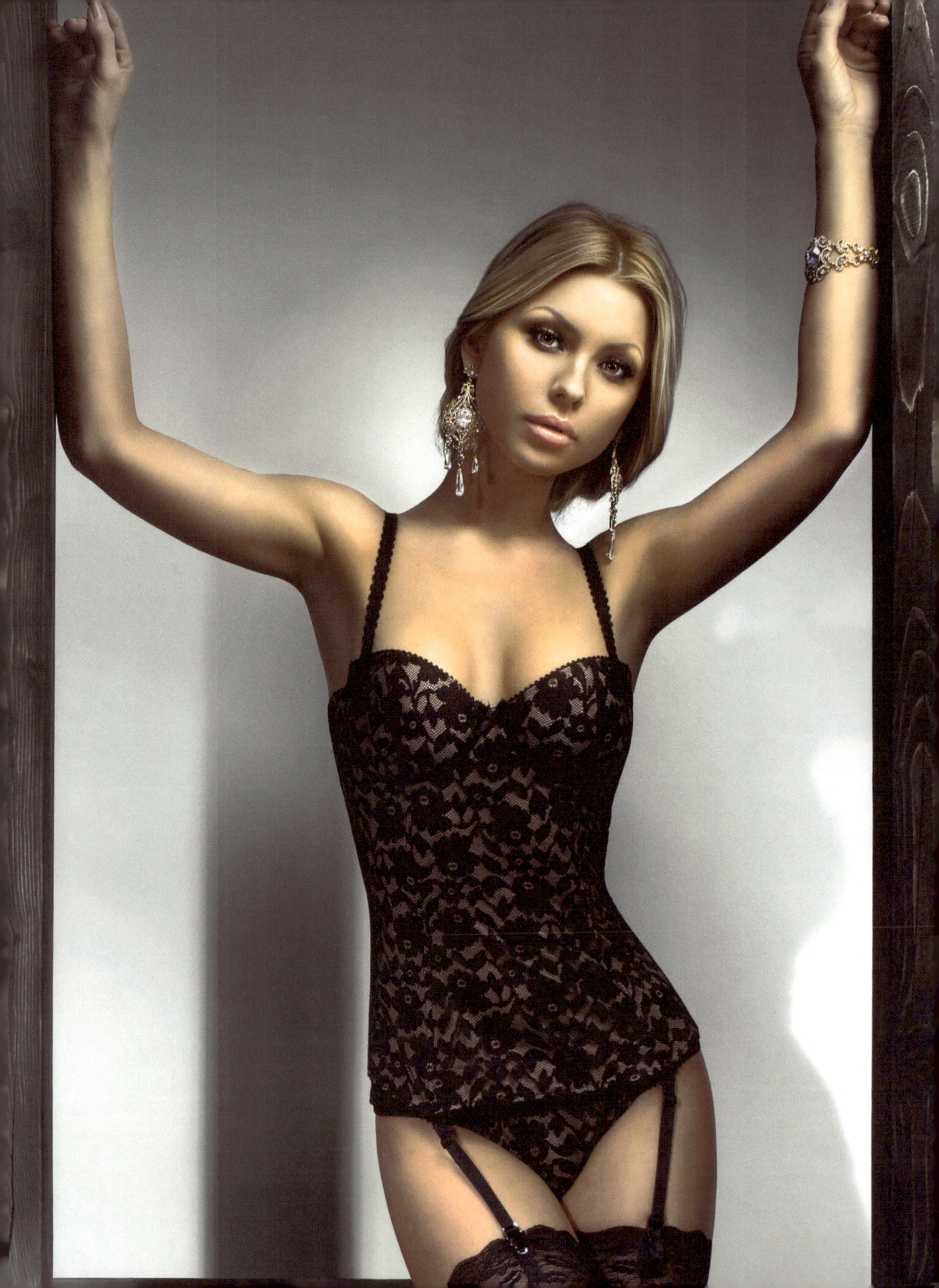

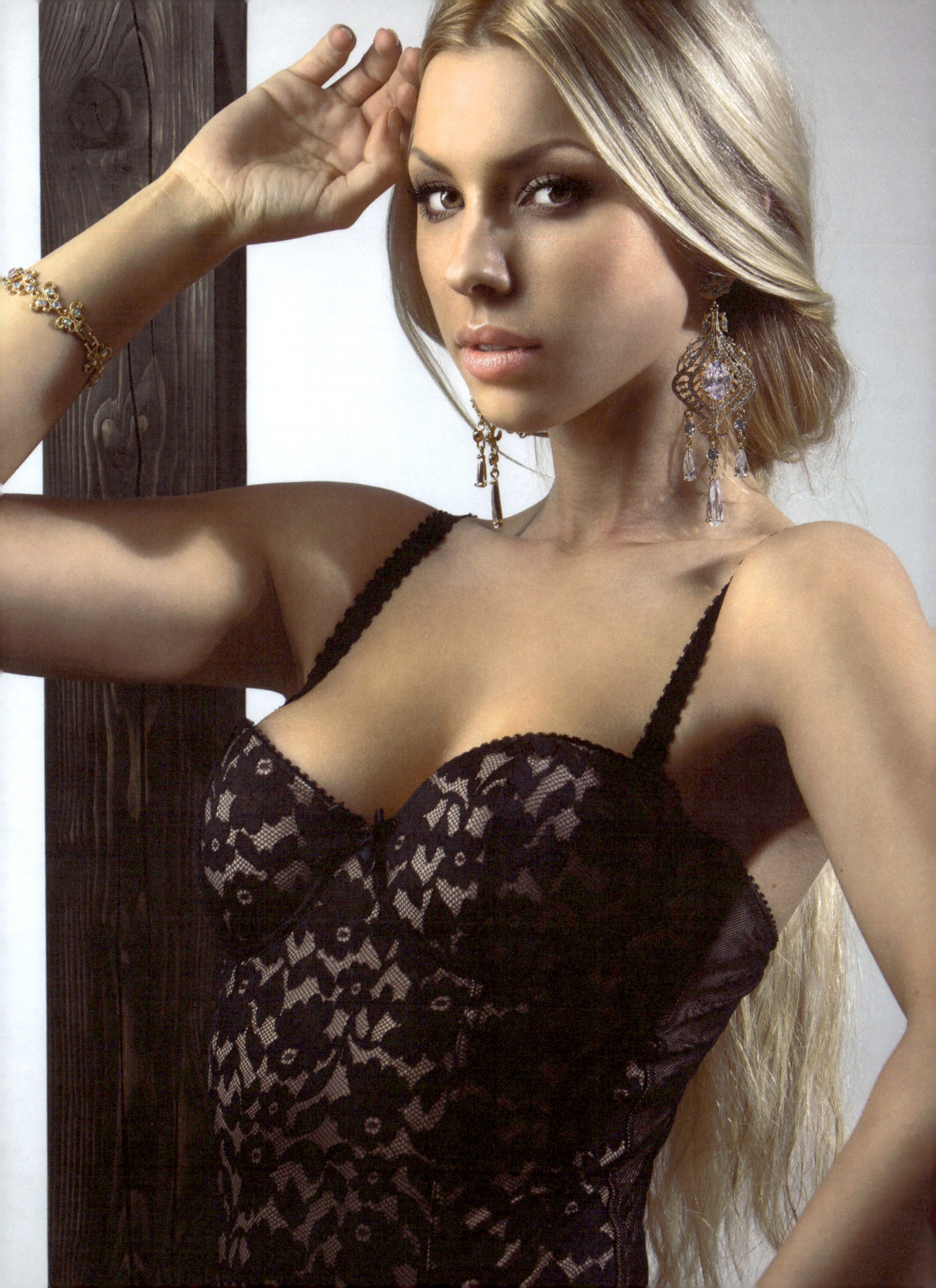

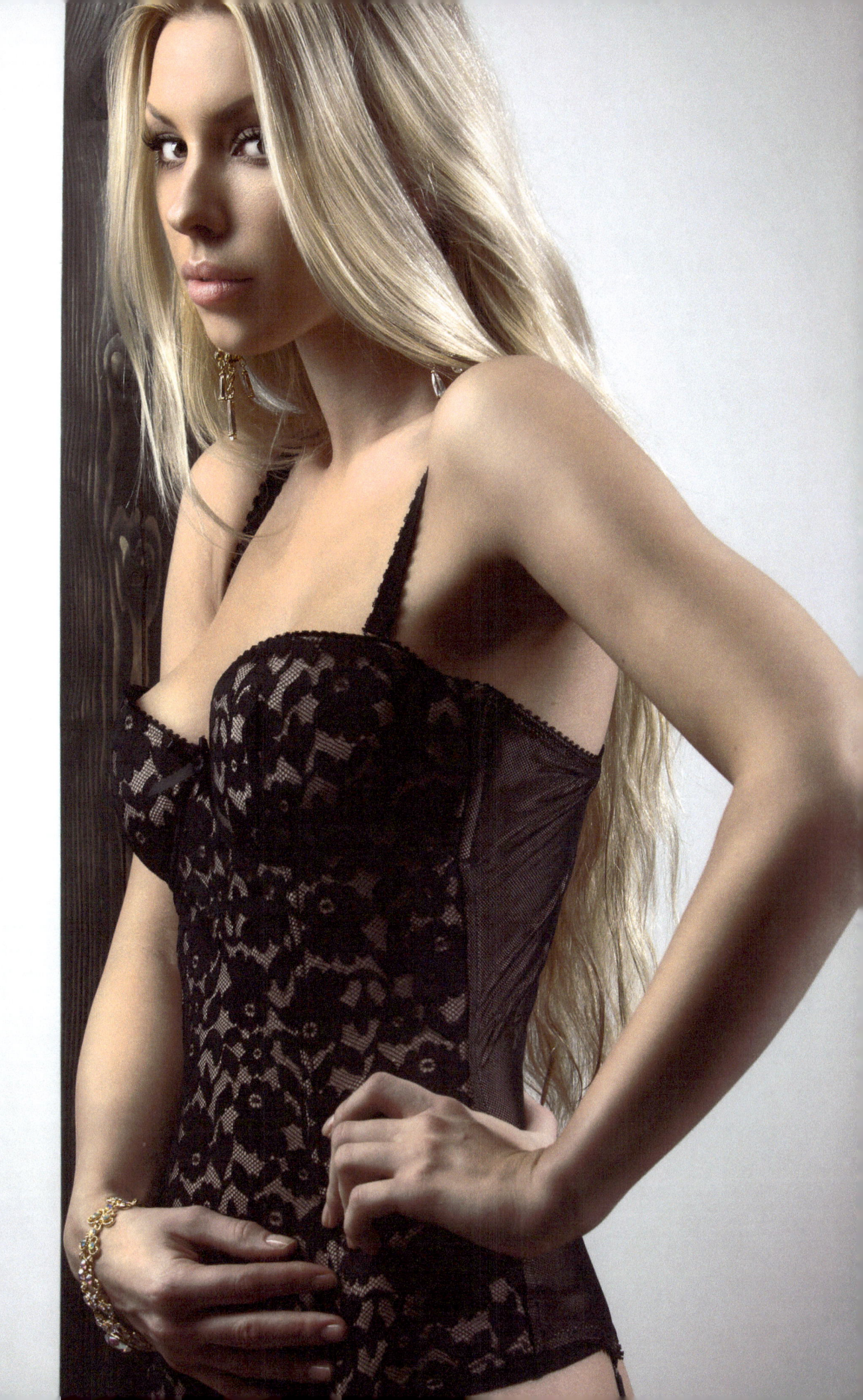

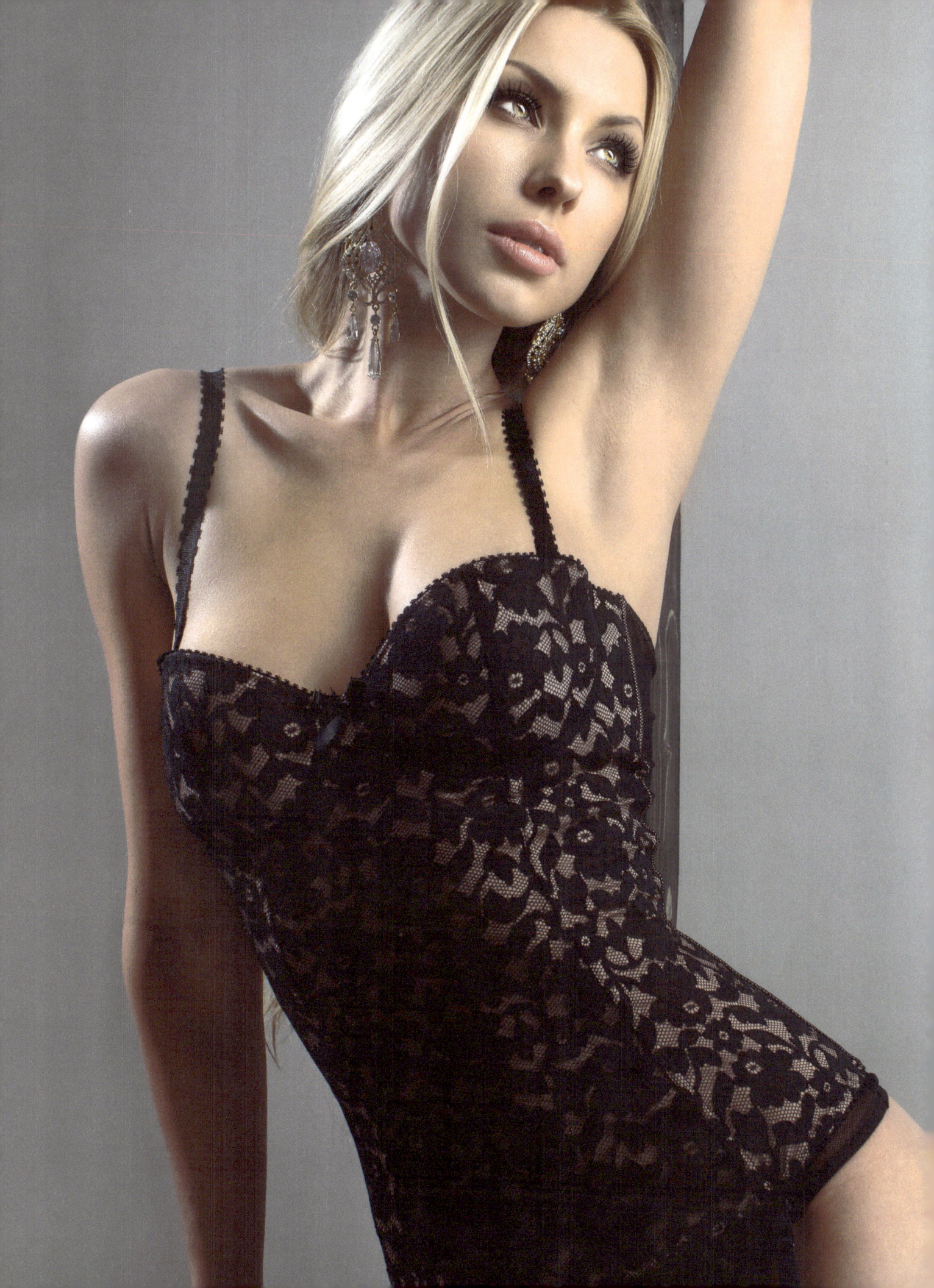

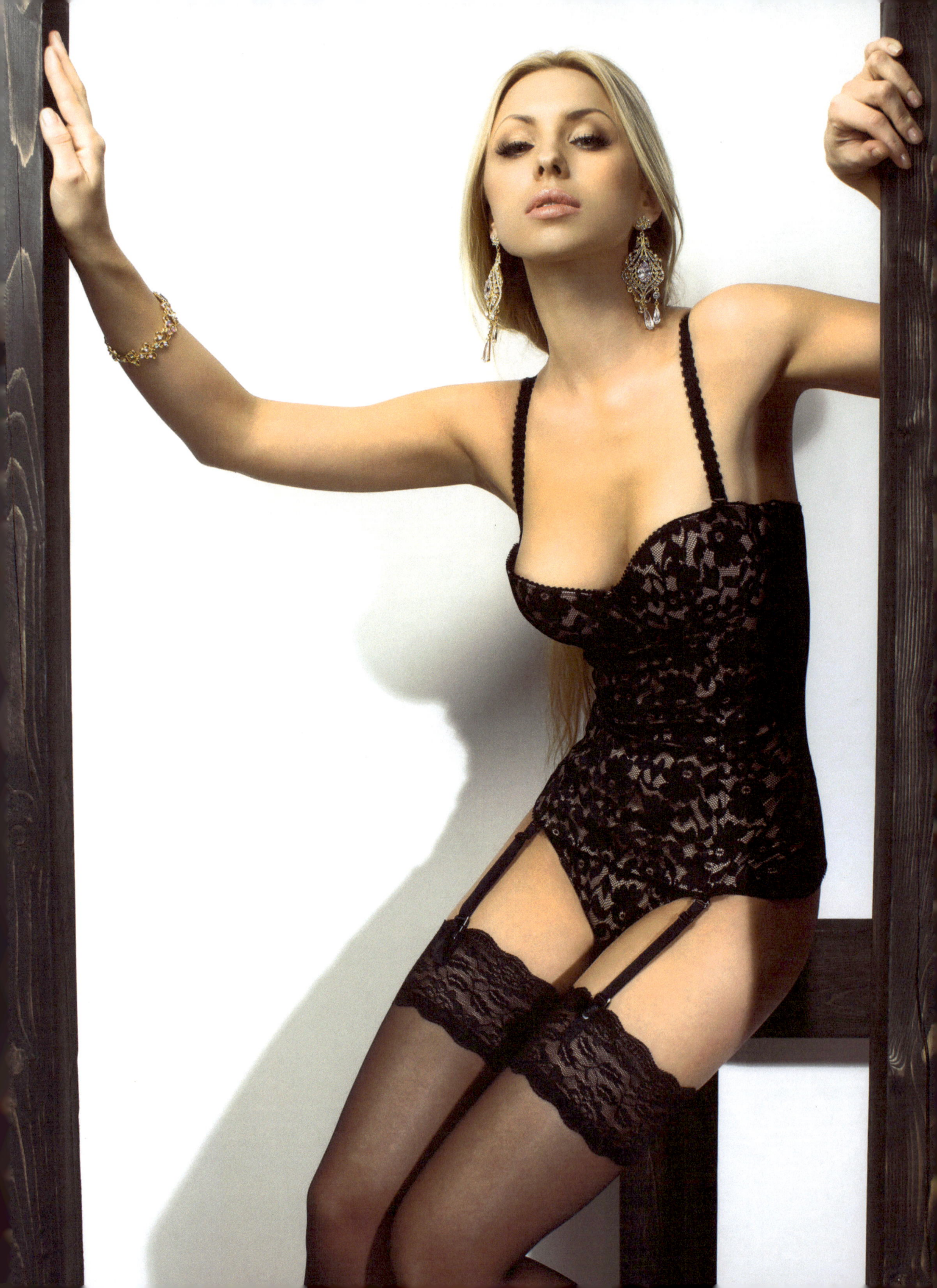

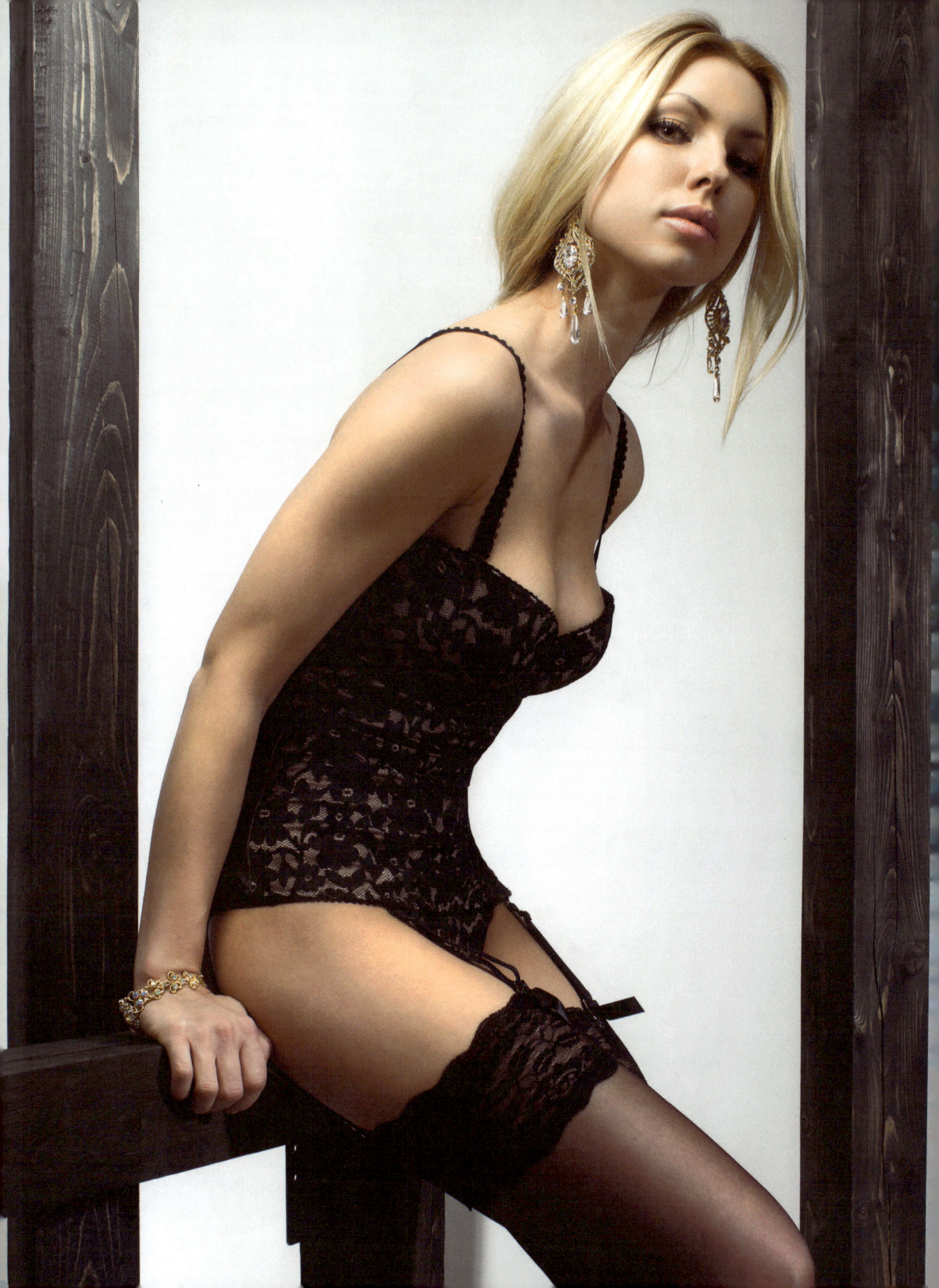

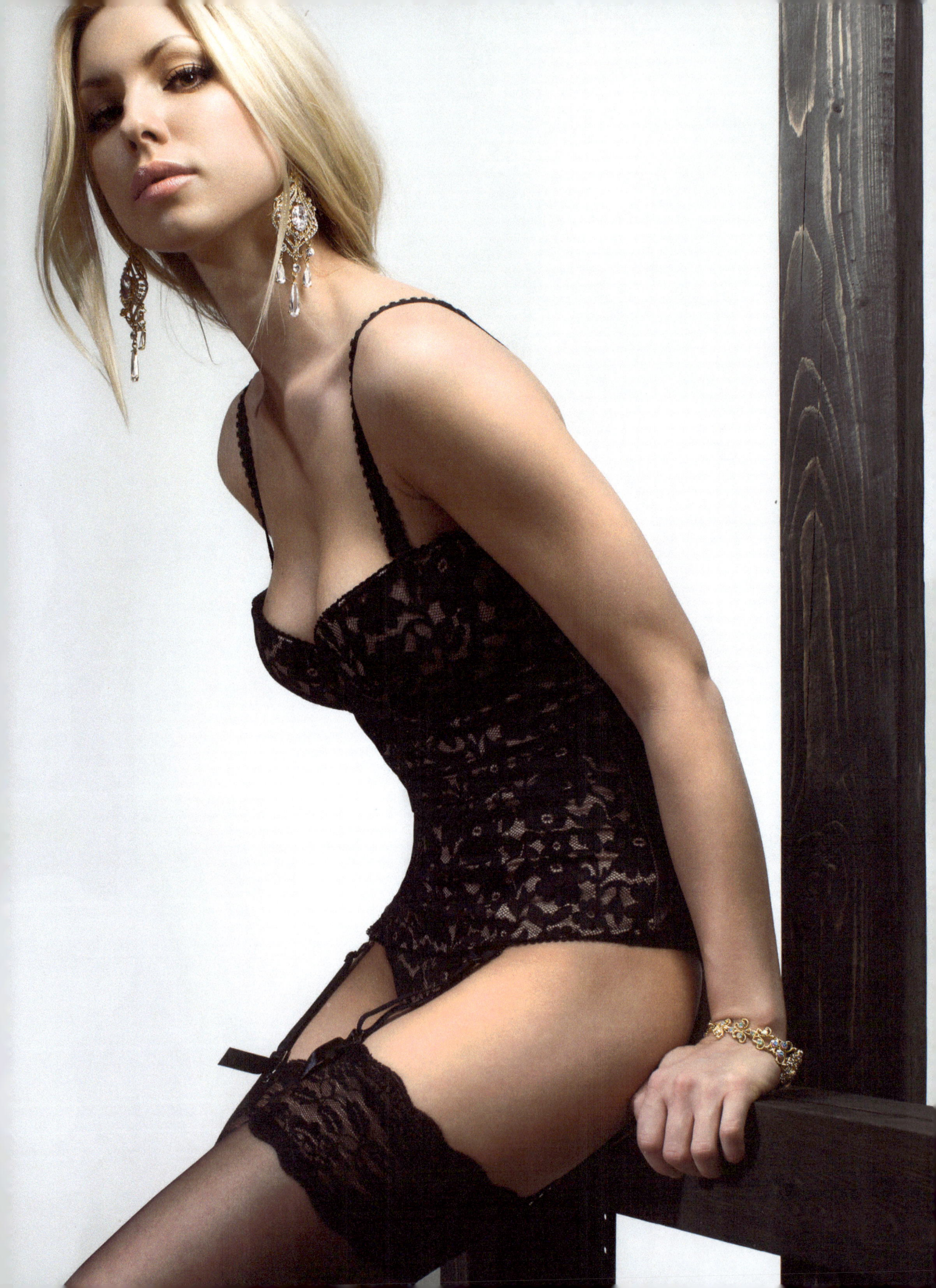

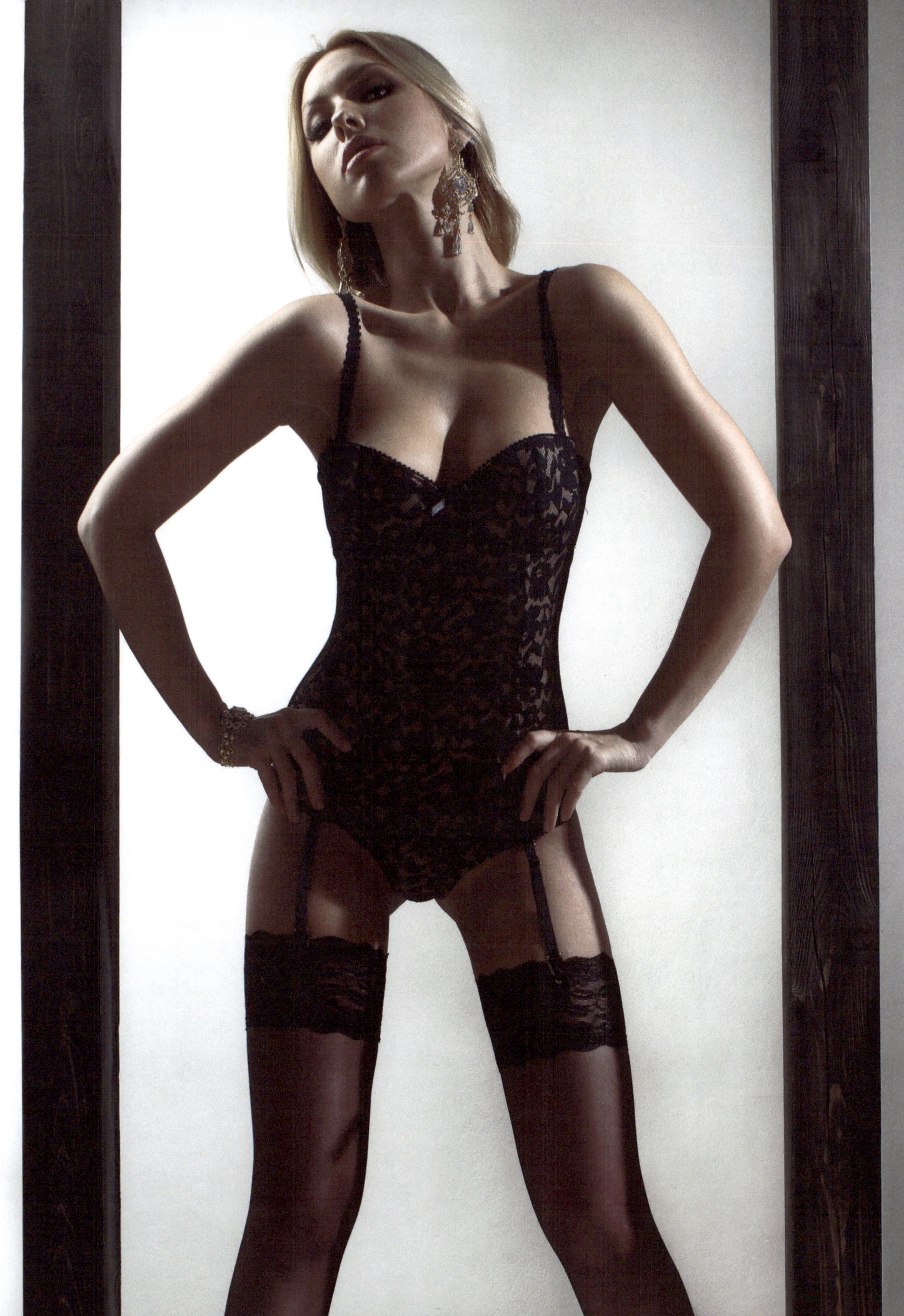

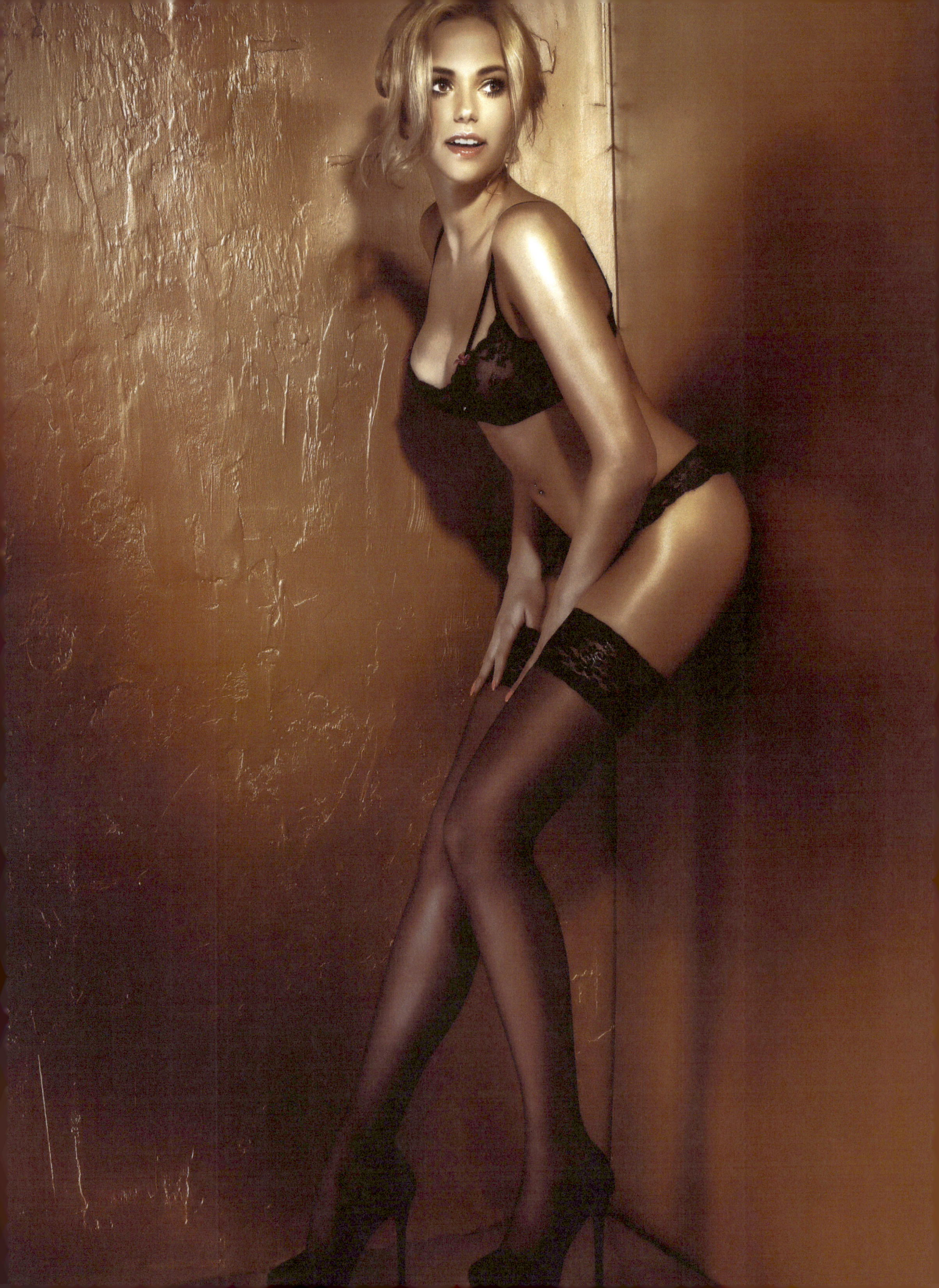

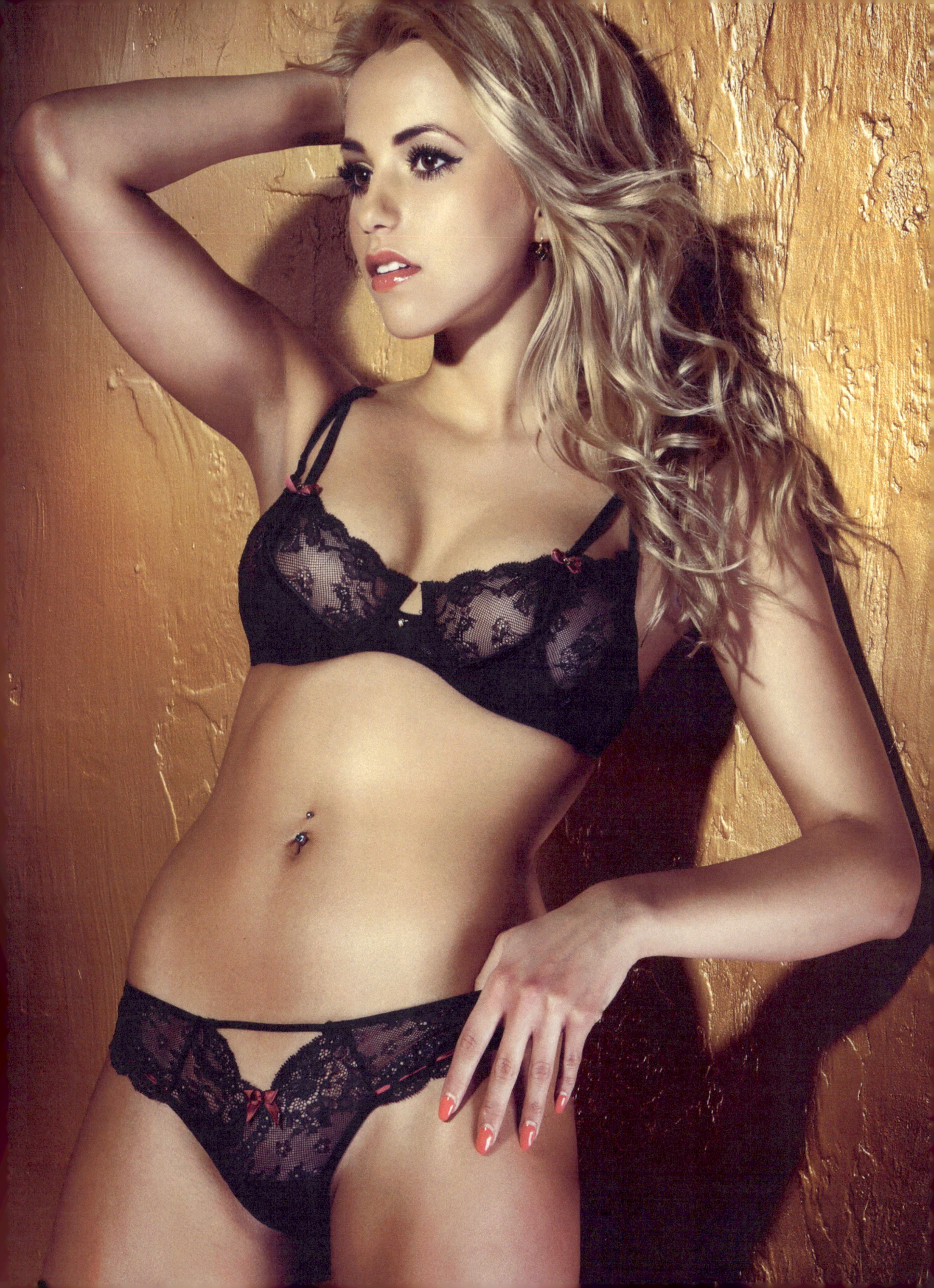

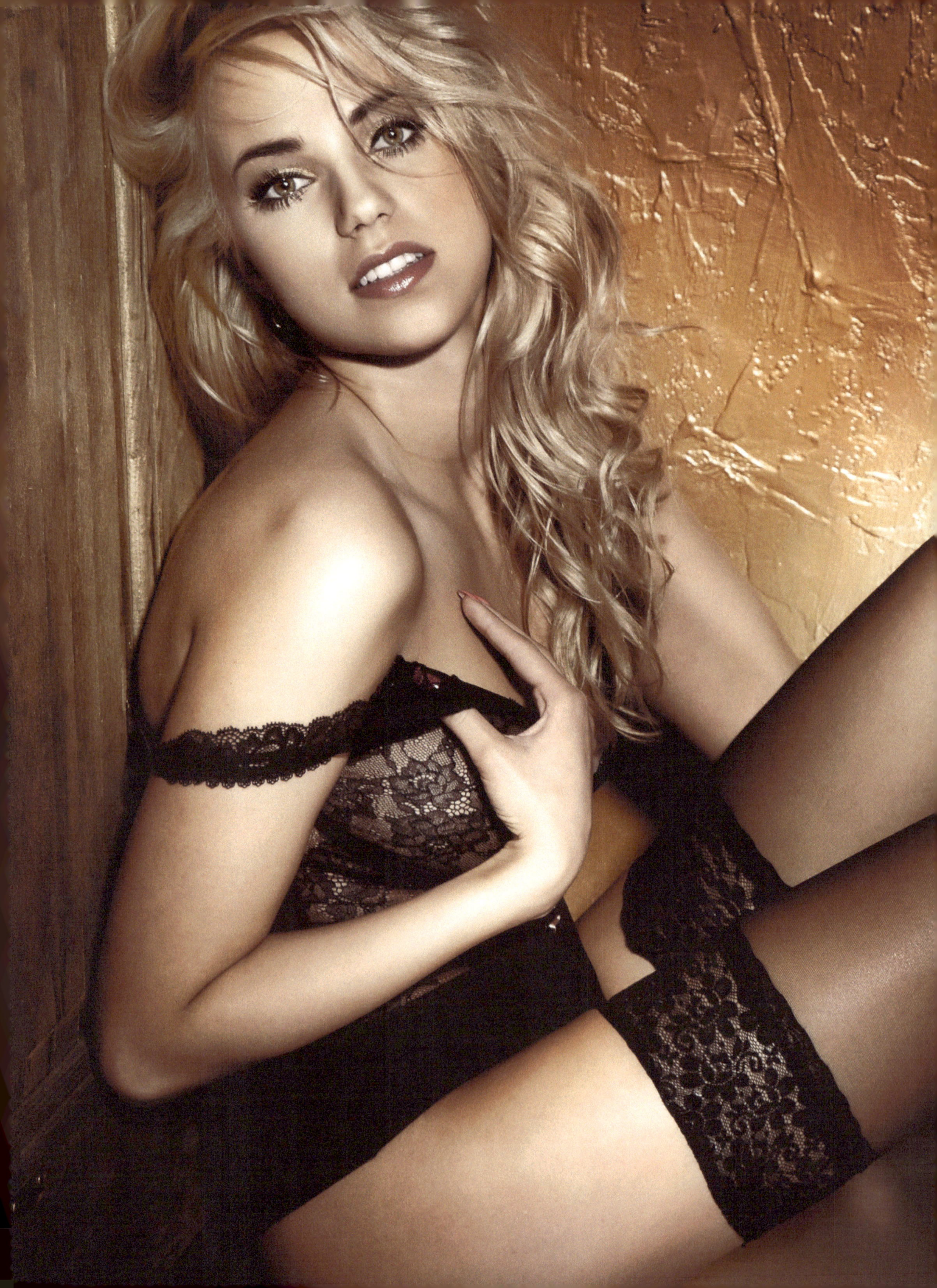

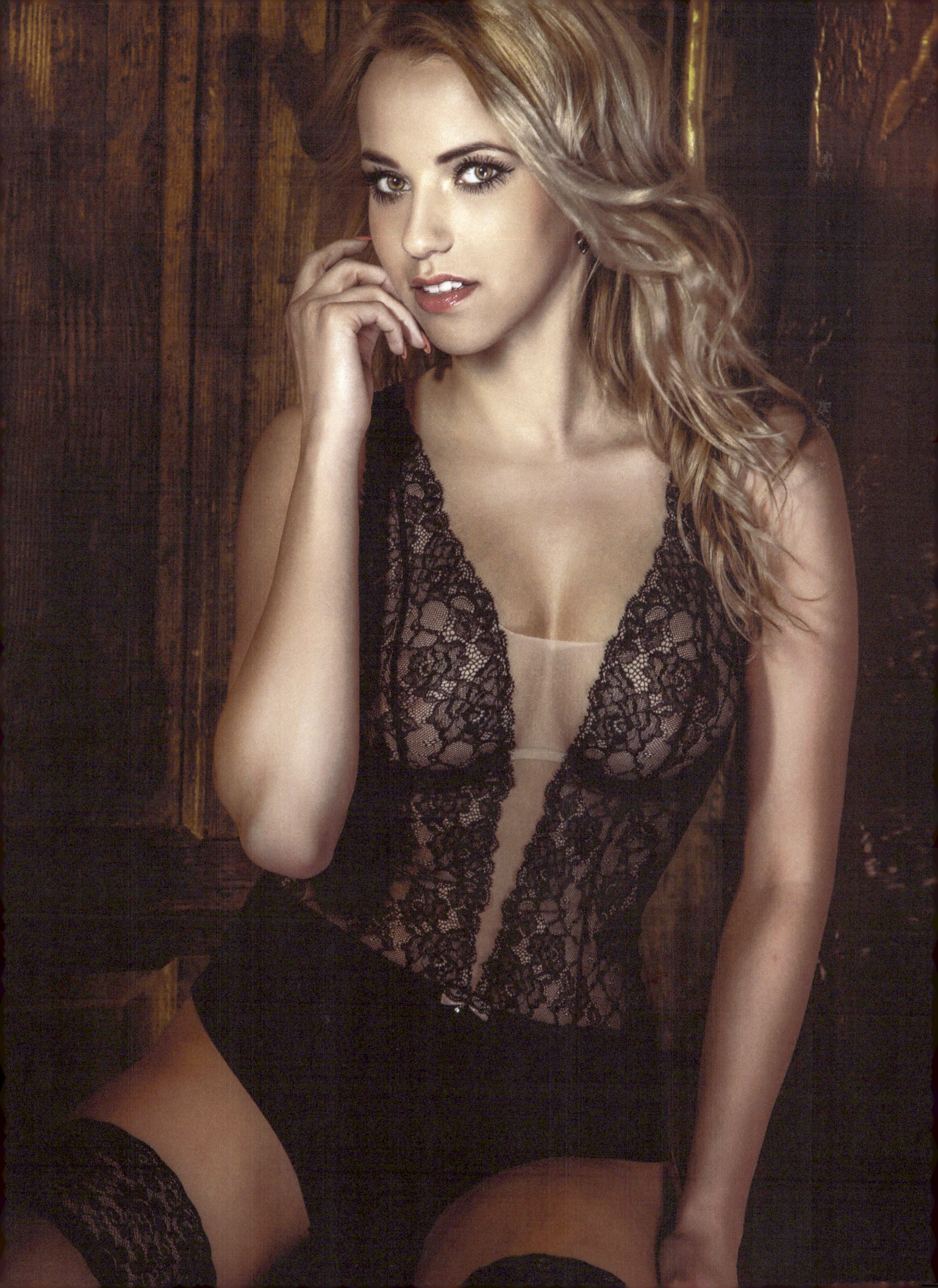

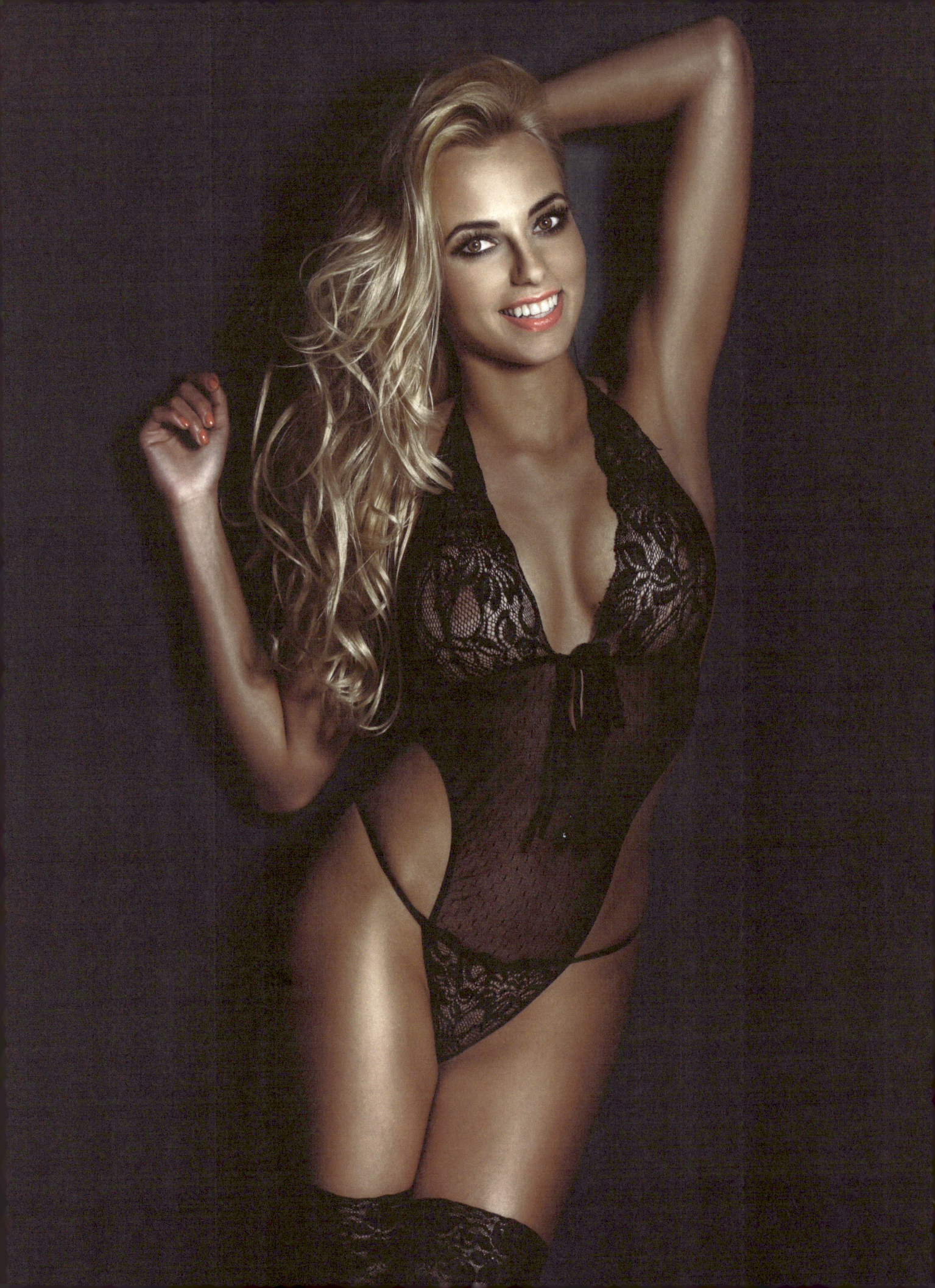

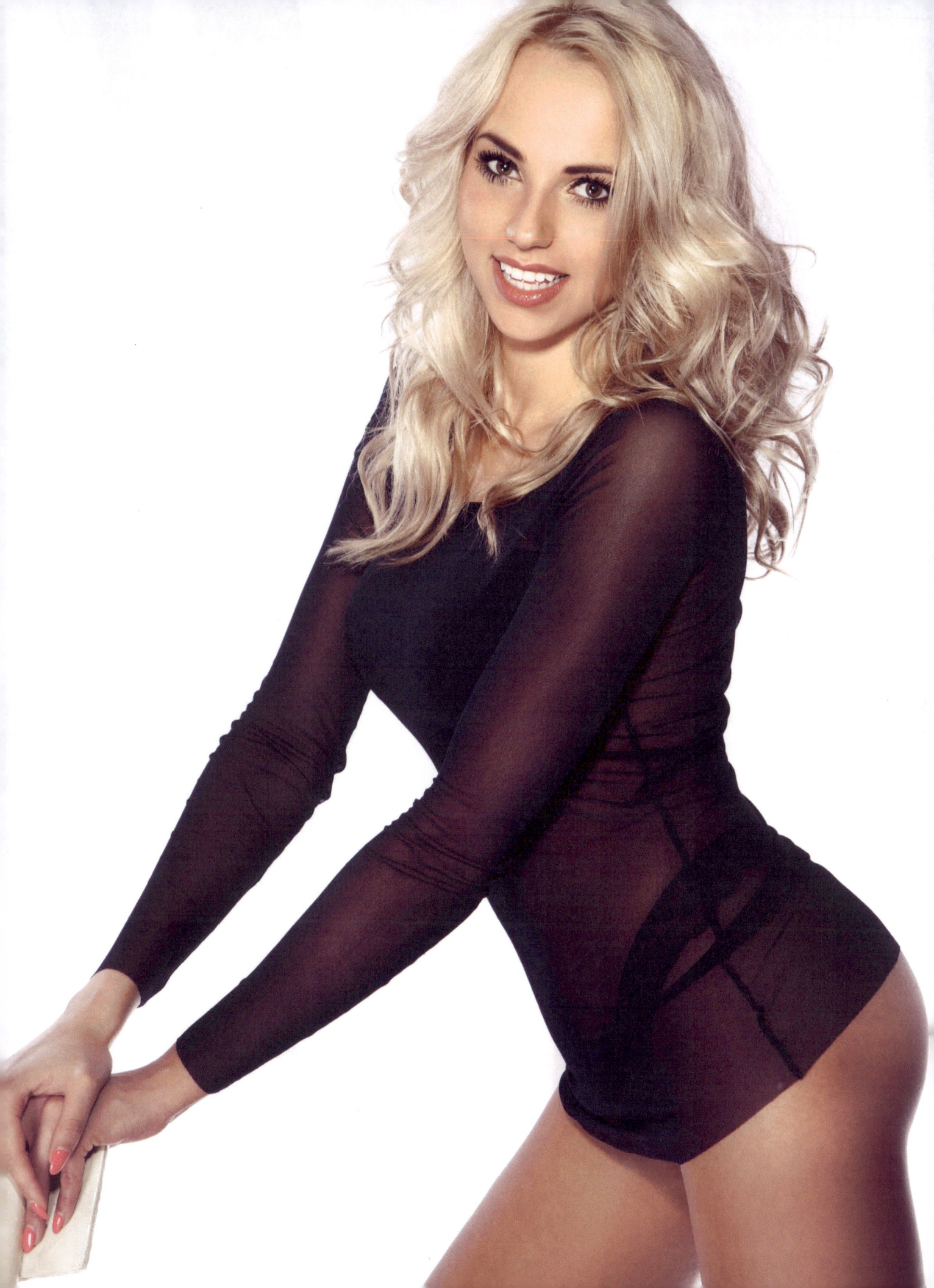

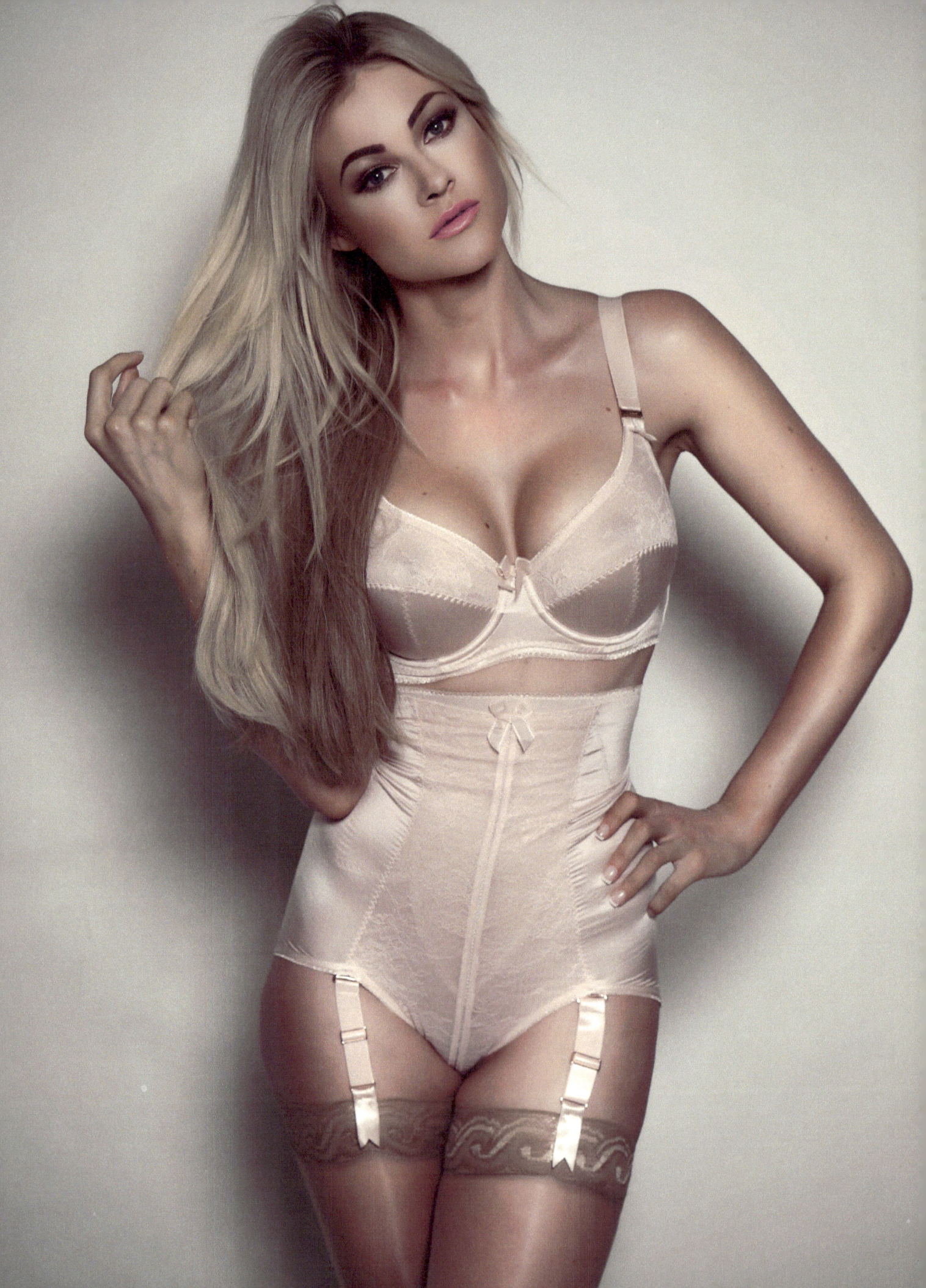

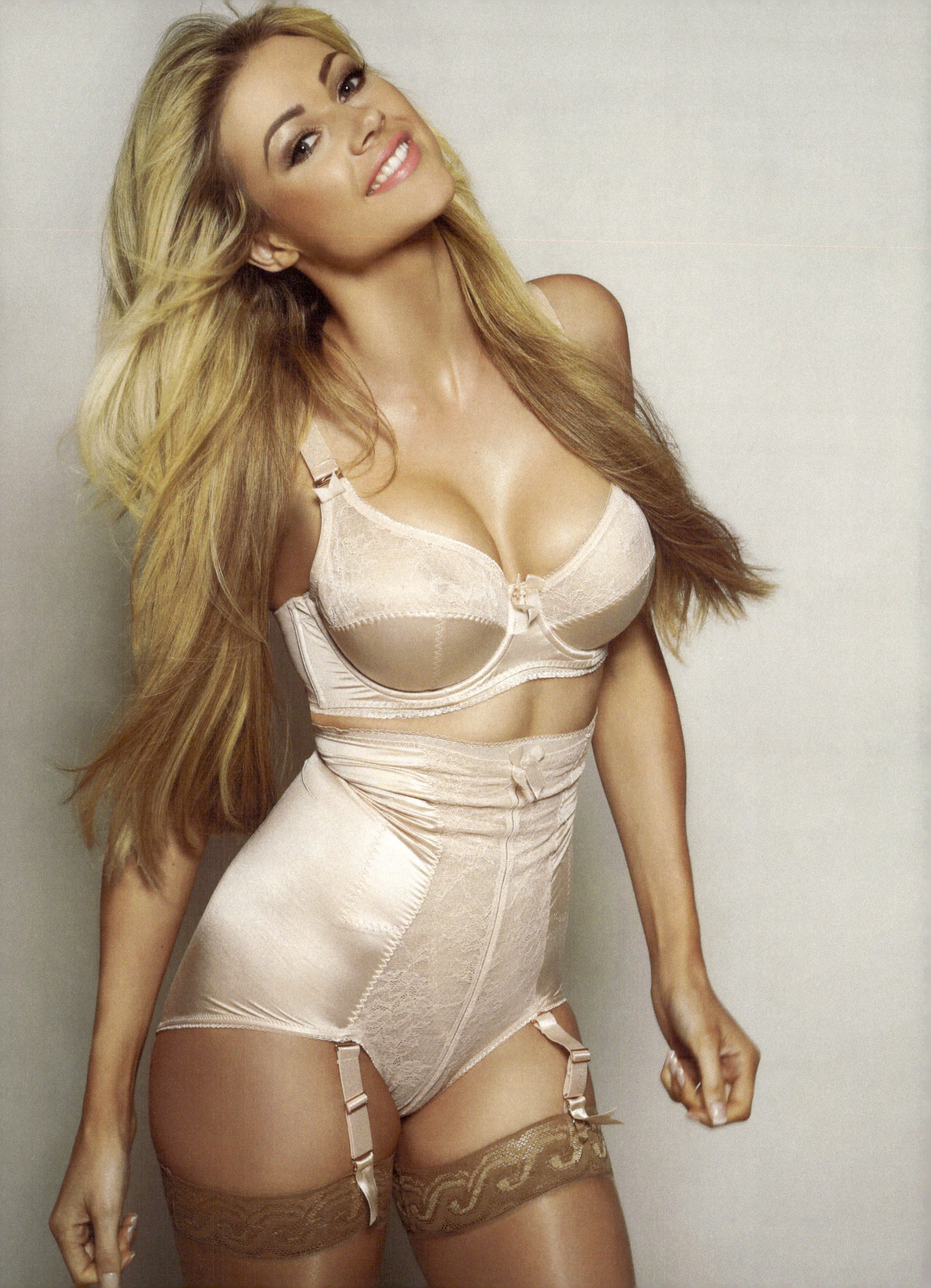

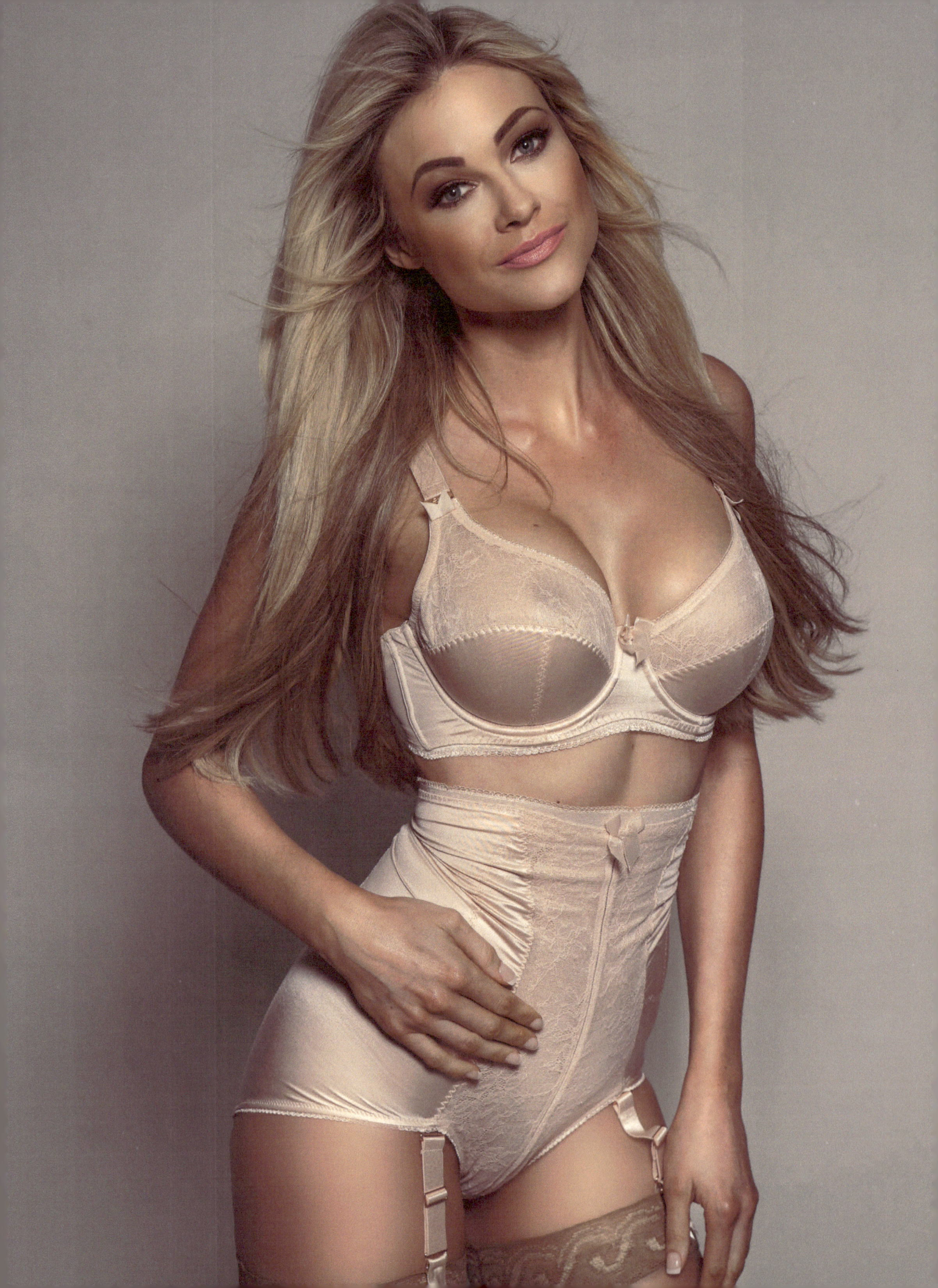

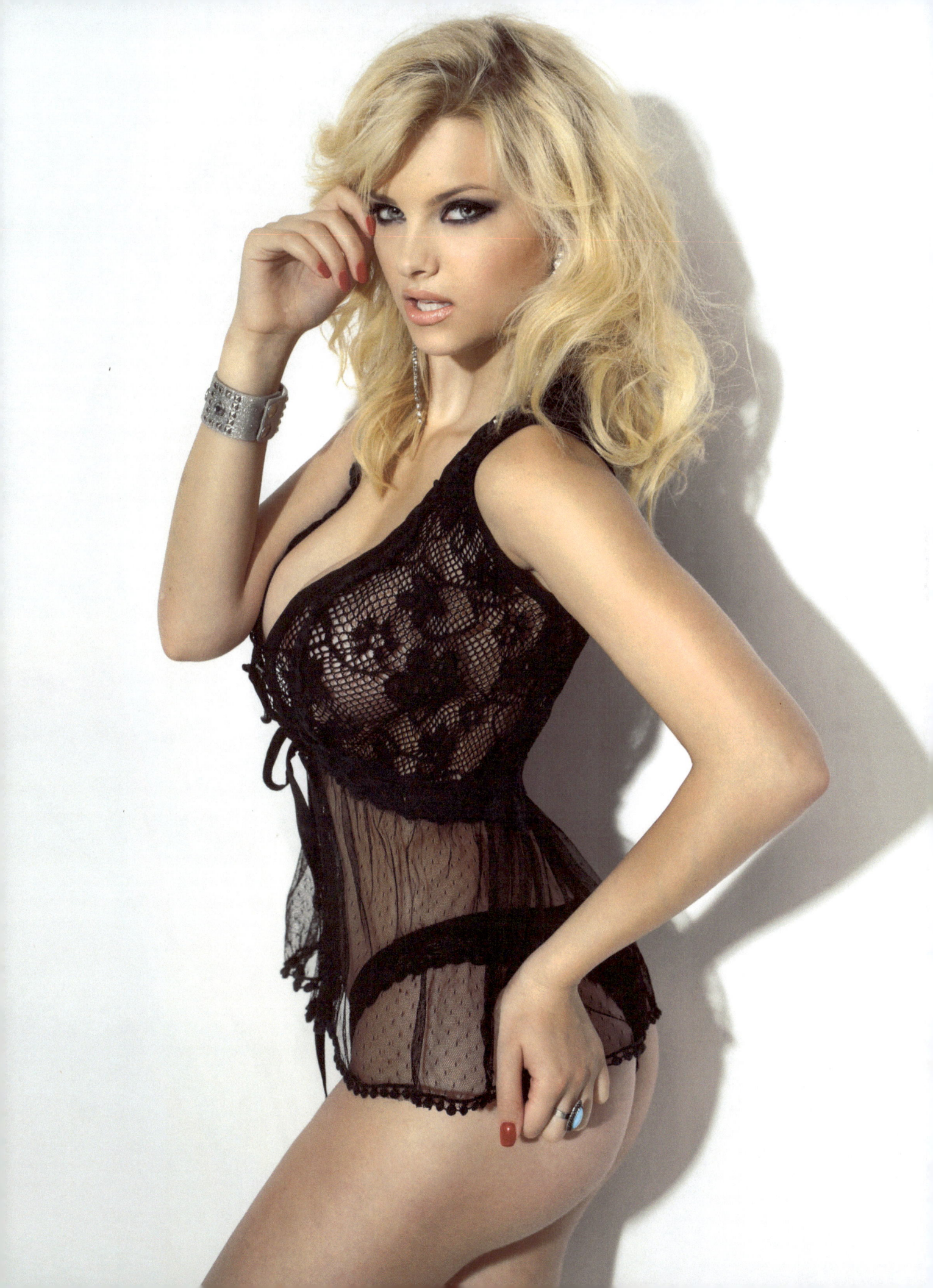

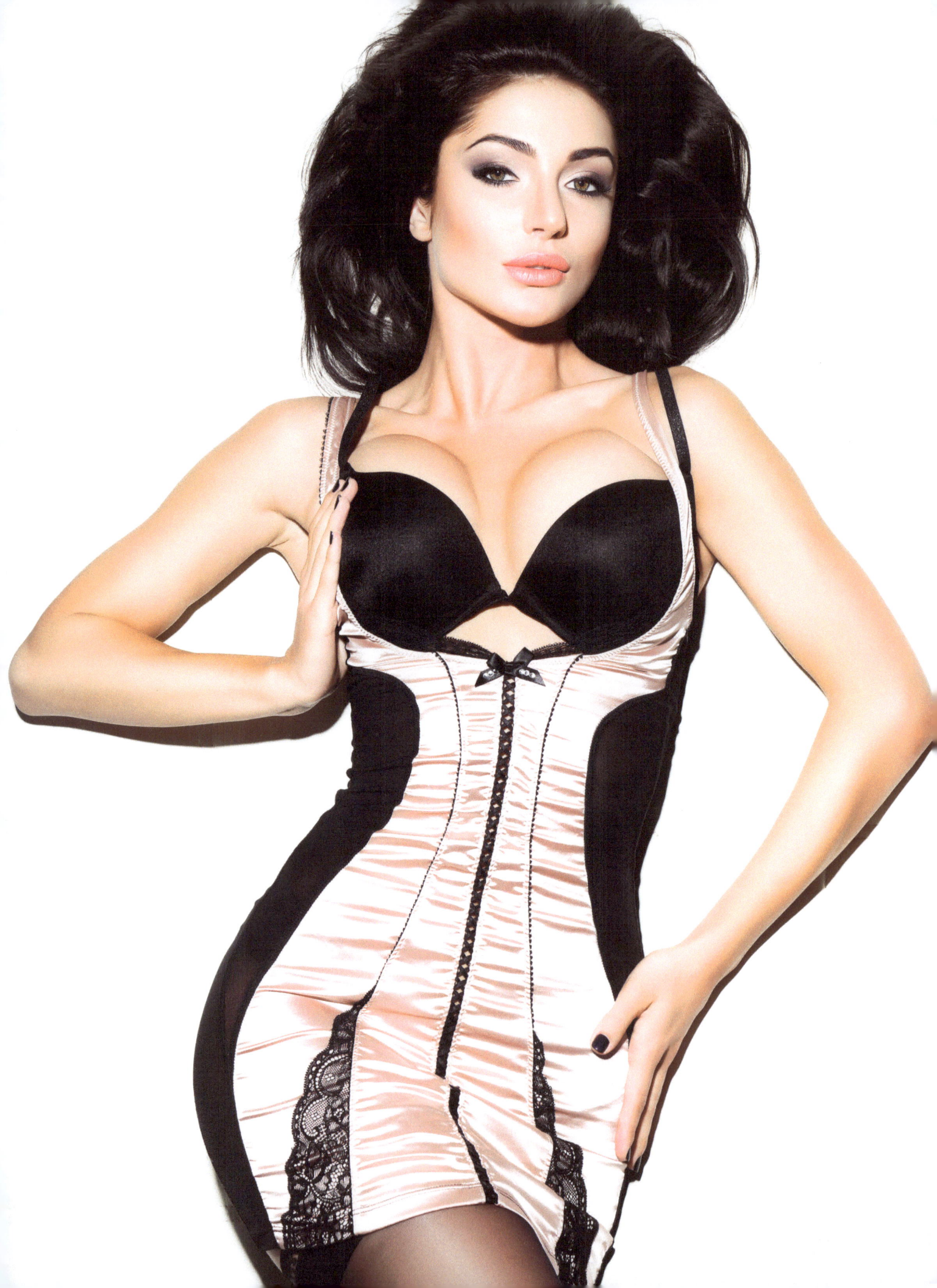

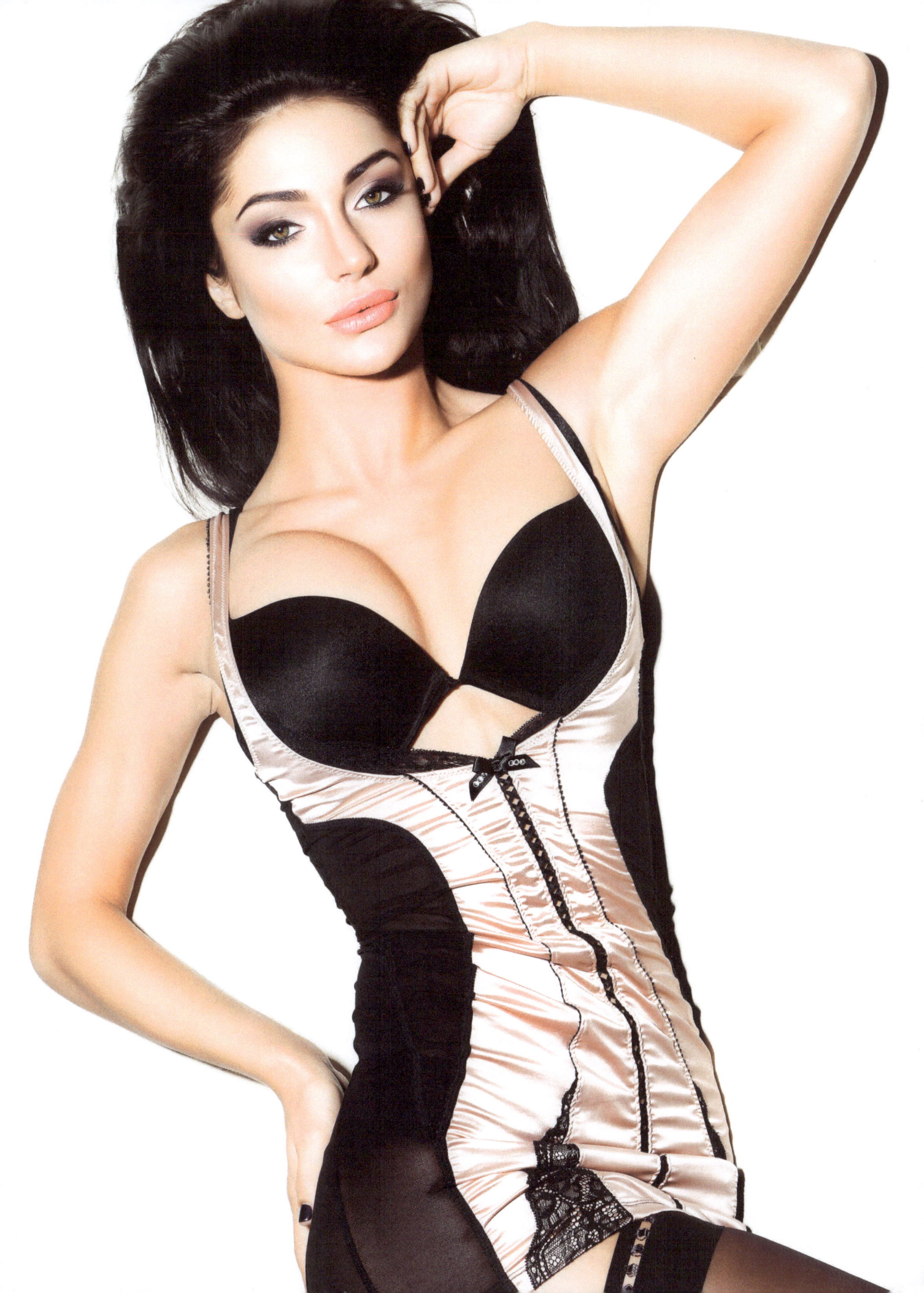

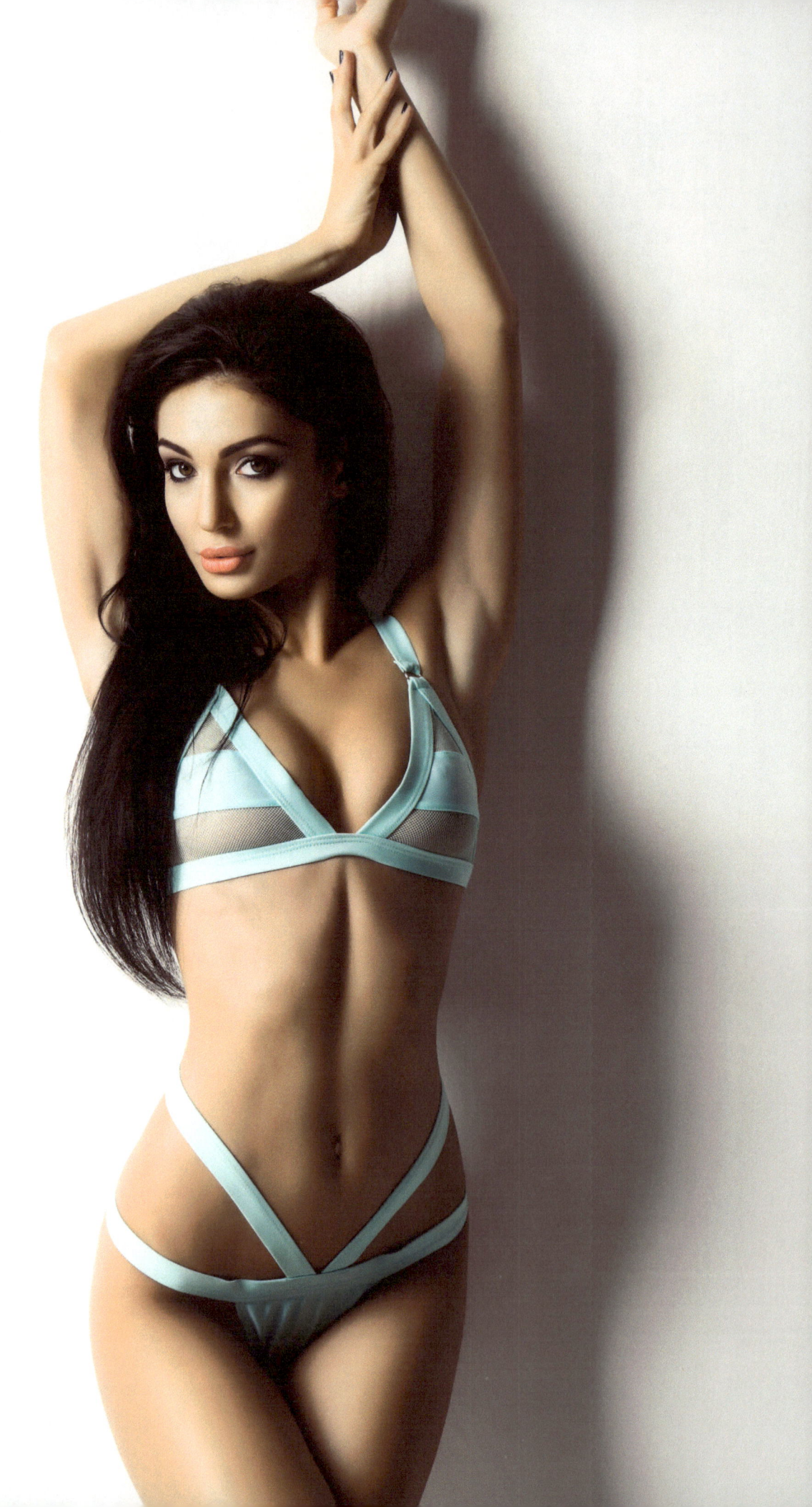

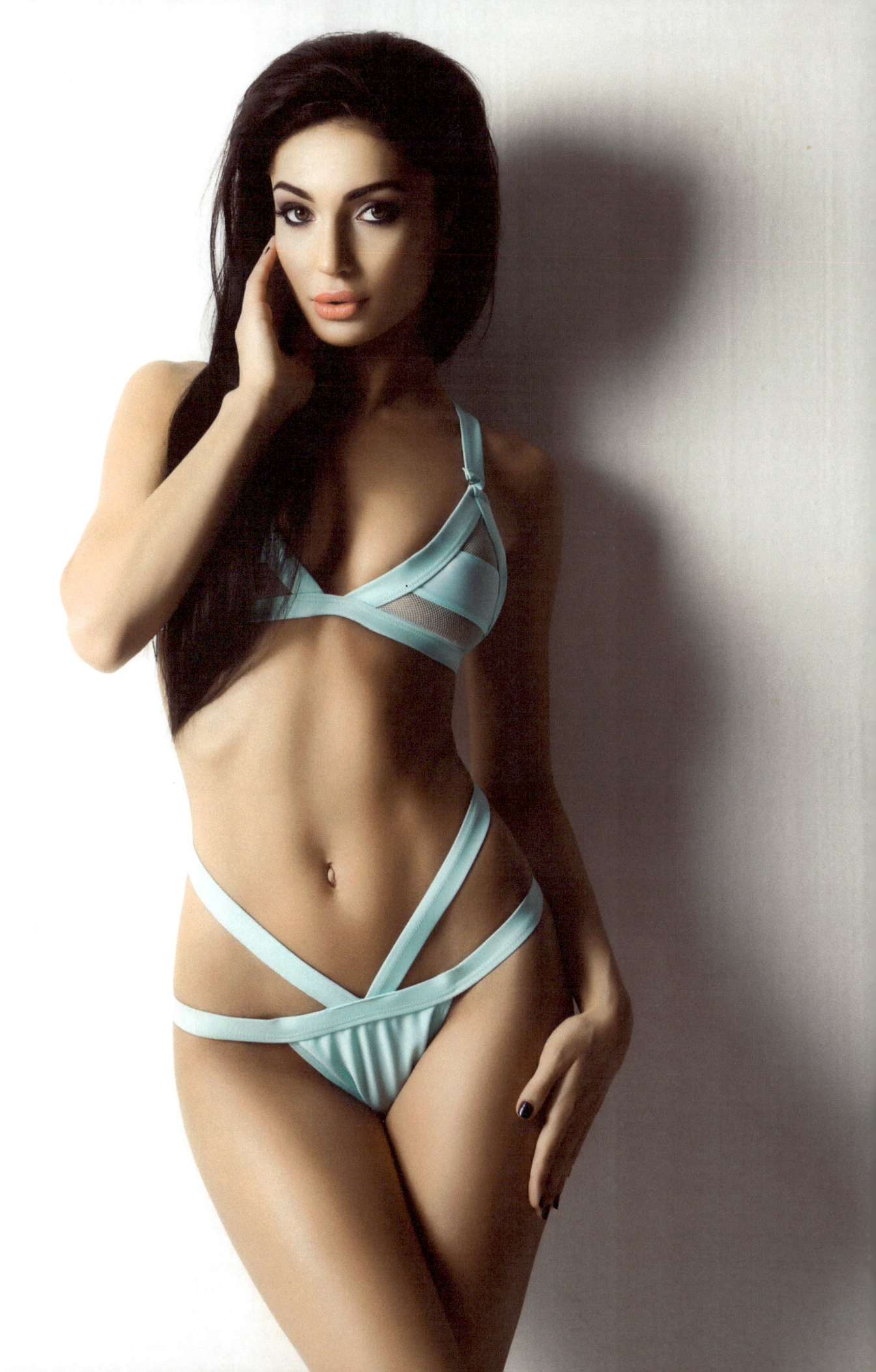

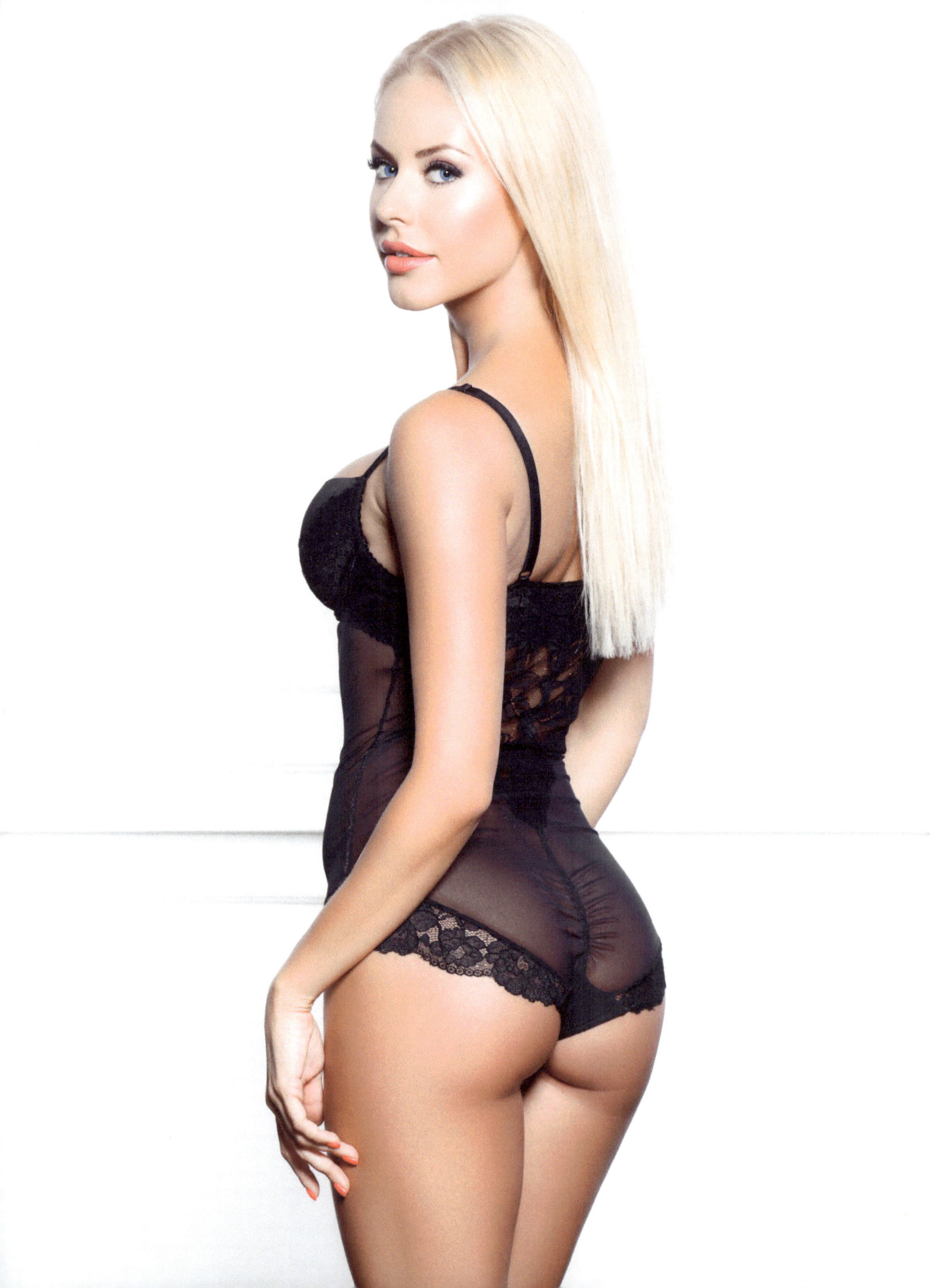

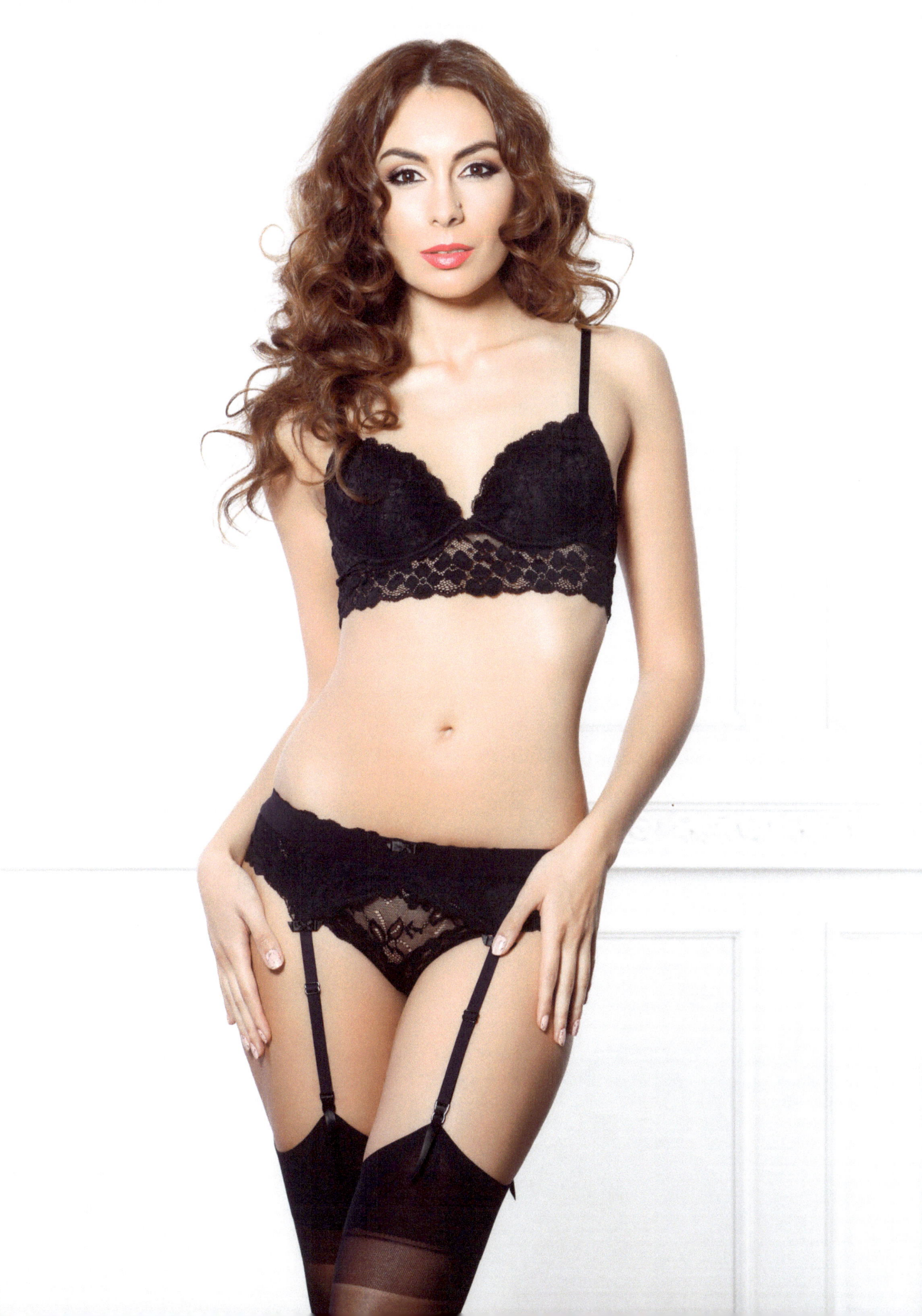

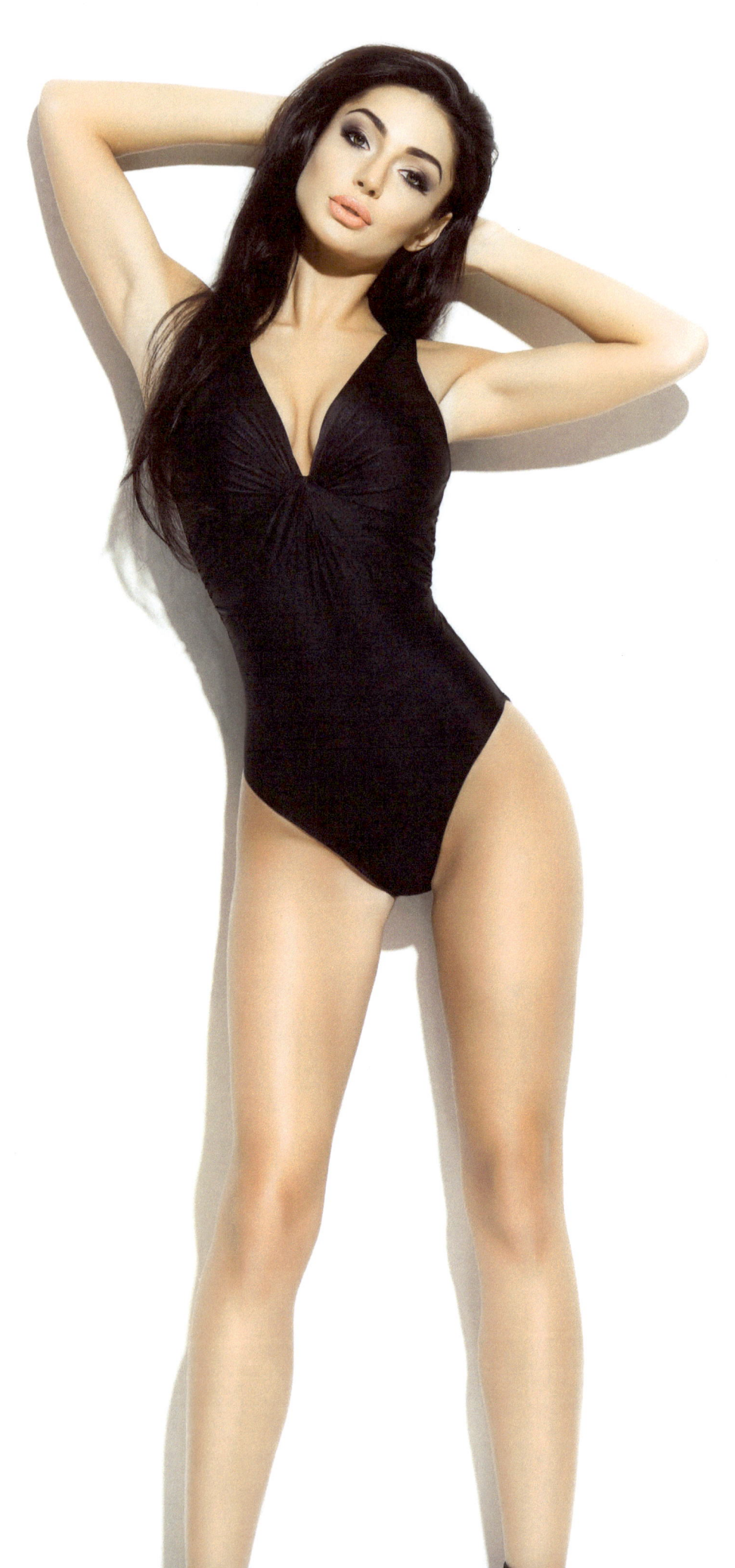

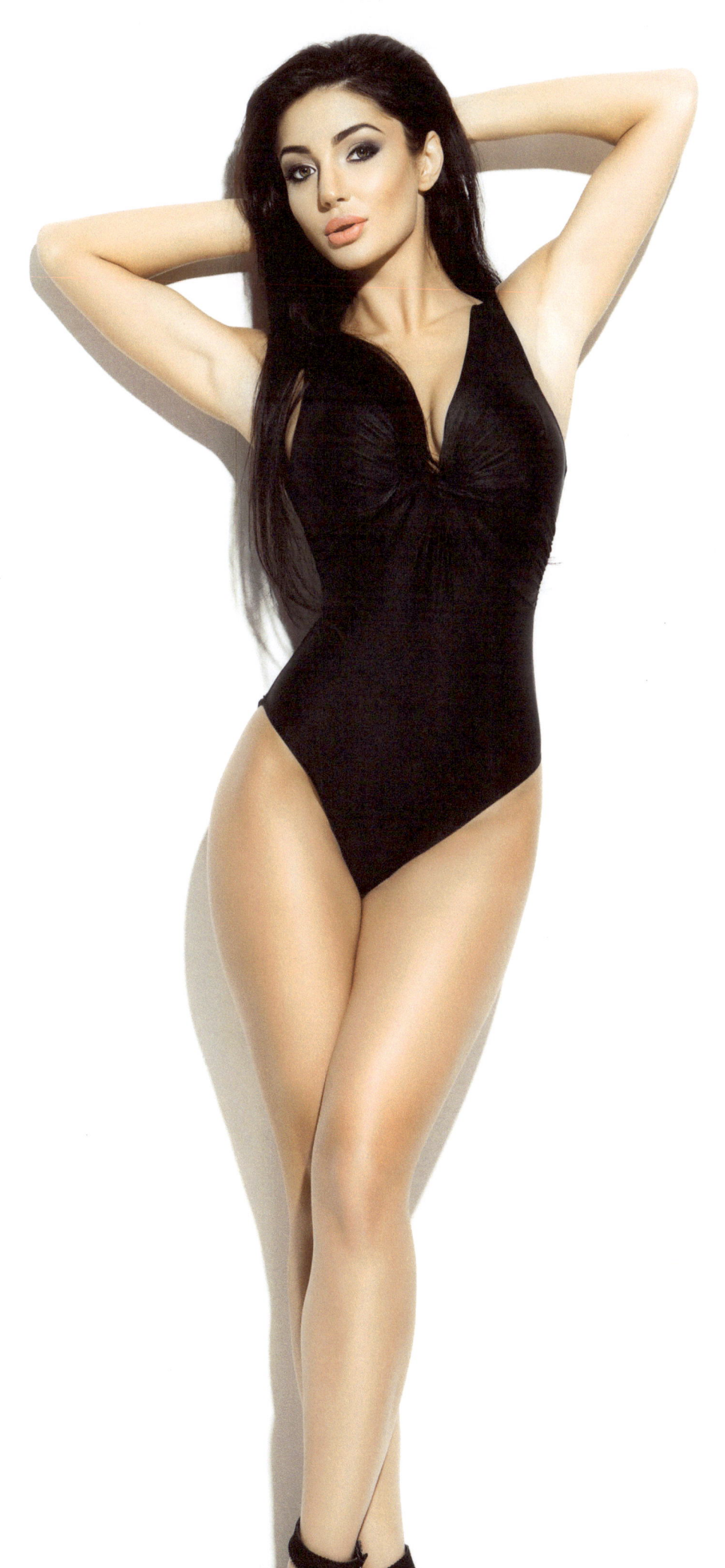

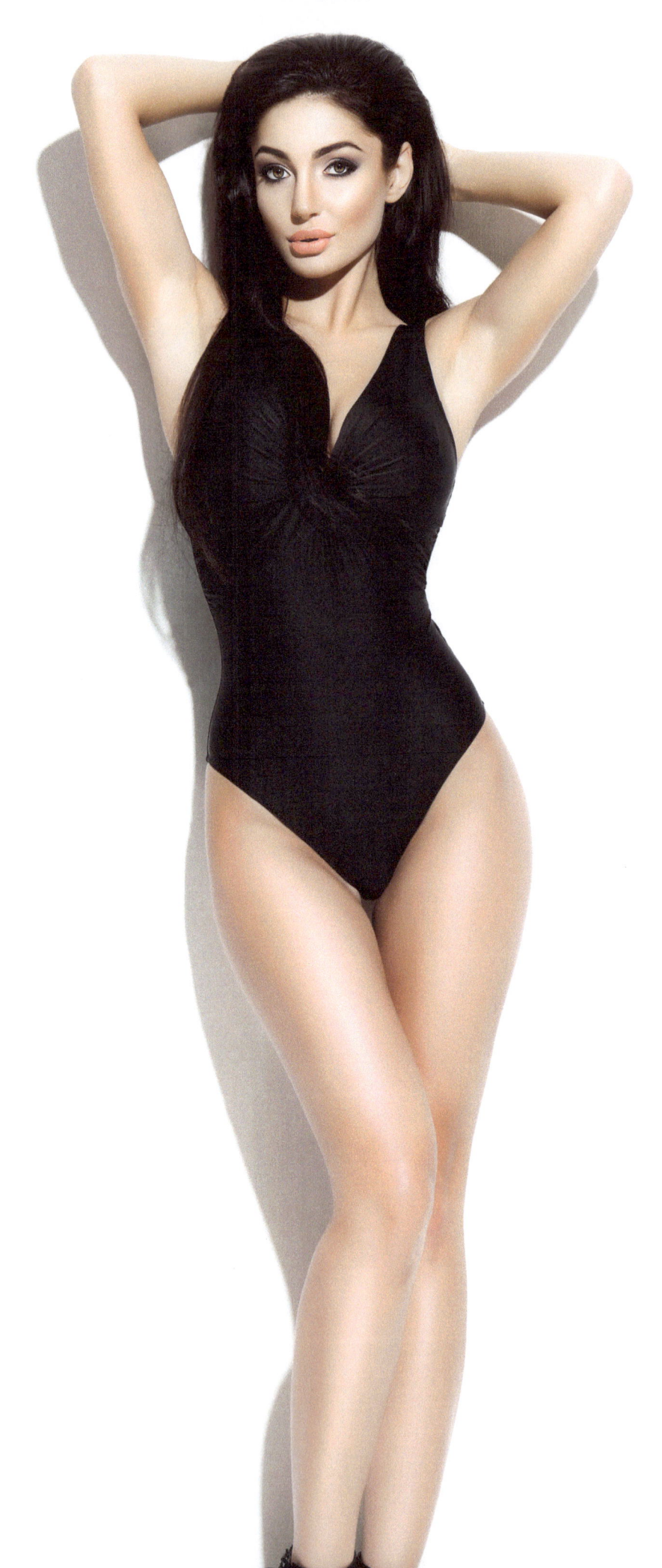

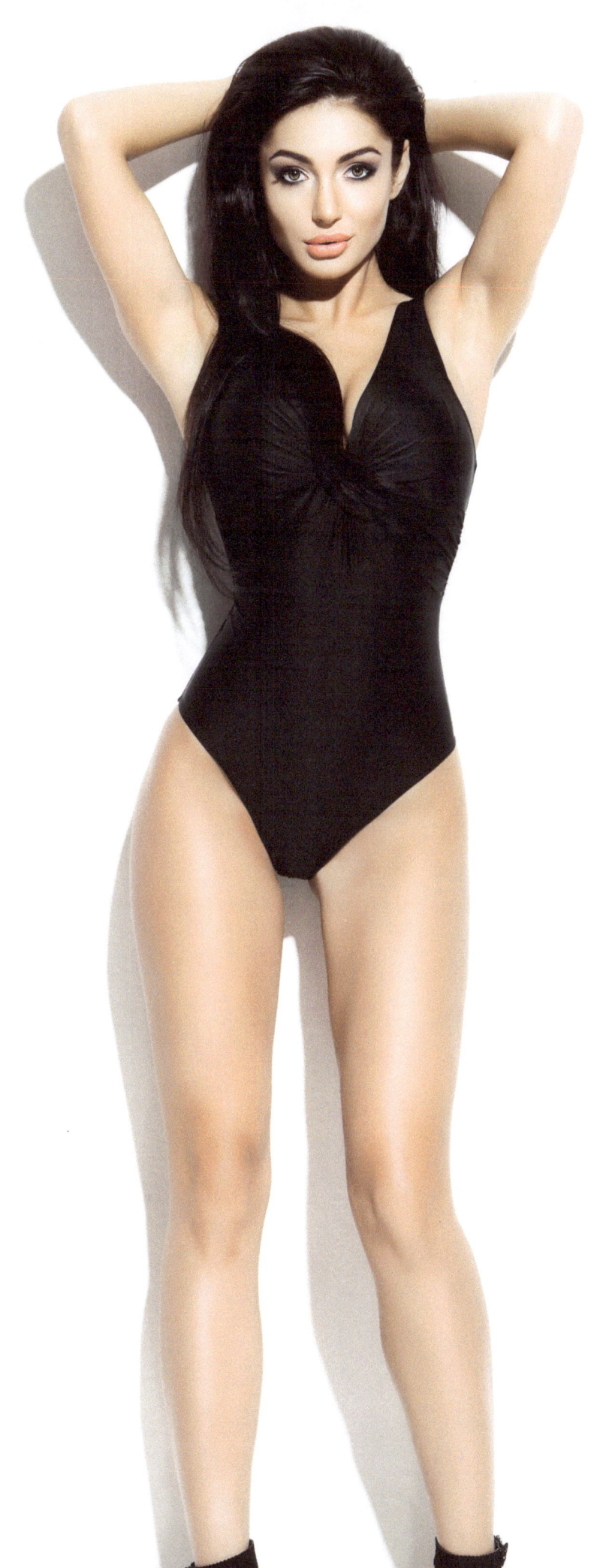

www.ingramcontent.com/pod-product-compliance
Lightning Source LLC
Chambersburg PA
CBHW040754200526
45159CB00025B/2386